Freelancing Secrets

(Vol. 1)

'Setting Up Work Environment'

Vivek Nayyar

OHGOI
www.ohgoi.com

DISCLAIMER

Although 'Setting Up Work Environment' and all the volumes of 'Freelancing Secrets' series explain the processes and ethics that should be followed to get a good paying career, they do not guarantee the success of the readers.

The author, the publisher, or the team members of OHGOI are not liable, and in any manner, should not be held responsible for any controversies or losses that the readers might face by following the suggestions given in this book whatsoever. Any results – positive or negative – that the readers may experience by following the guidelines given in this book would be their own responsibility.

PREFACE

'Freelancing Secrets' is a series of multiple volumes.

Understanding the increased employees' exploitation in today's world, and the latest trend of freelancing the office workers are getting inclined to, the whole idea of 'Freelancing Secrets' is to provide step-by-step guidance and to suggest the freelancing ethics to those who are planning to quit their jobs and start their own business.

Assuming that the readers are office employees and know nothing about freelancing, starting from the scratch, 'Setting Up Work Environment' – this particular volume of the 'Freelancing Secrets' series – covers in detail and with reasons what preparations are needed and how to get started with the freelancing business with minimal investment and least efforts.

Likewise, the complete 'Freelancing Secrets' series explains in details and with reasons the business ethics, communication tactics, the ways a freelancer should interact with the clients to get the projects from them and gain good reputation, and the methods to work effectively and efficiently while equally balancing his or her professional and personal lives at the same time.

In all, 'Freelancing Secrets' covers every aspect of the transition of the reader's career from an office employee to having a handsomely paying freelancing career, and then continuing the journey toward becoming a successful entrepreneur.

By the time you have read all the volumes of the 'Freelancing Secrets' series, you can expect to: a) Know most, if not all, requirements and ethics of becoming a successful freelancer, and b) Know the ingredients needed to become an entrepreneur.

Your honest and impartial feedbacks are always welcome.

Regards

Vivek Nayyar

vivek.nayyar@ohgoi.com

OHGOI

www.ohgoi.com

Who Should Read This Book?

Anyone who:

> - Is not satisfied with his or her job.
> - Is not satisfied with the remuneration he or she gets in the regular 8 hours' job.
> - Has the feeling of being exploited by the seniors/employers.
> - Has innovative ideas but they are not entertained or honored by the others.
> - Believes that his or her potential and skills are not worth wasting in the 9-to-5 job.
> - Wants to earn some extra cash.
> - Has big dreams and is ready to work hard to make them come true, but is looking for the right guidance to get started.

If you belong to any one or more of the above categories, this book and all the other volumes that it follows are for you.

In 'Setting Up Work Environment' you will learn not only about setting up your office before you start working as a freelancer, you'll also know how can you get mentally prepared for the freelancing business, what strategies should you follow to get a business plan, and even how deal with the stress and time crisis that you may face while working hard for your success.

CONTENTS AT A GLANCE

UNIT 1
SELF MOTIVATION

Scope of This Unit

As it is with every successful person, if you are trying something different, you are likely to face rejections, insults, and criticism from the people around you. If you are self-motivated, you need no encouragement from others, you won't even care about them, you will accept the rejections and criticisms as challenges, you will focus only and only on your target, and you will work hard to prove the critics wrong and become successful.

This unit explains how you can mentally prepare yourself to begin your career as a freelancer, leaving behind all the negatives that people may throw upon you.

Why Freelancing?

'Why Freelancing?' is the first and most important question that you must ask yourself before stepping into freelancing business.

By following the guidelines given in this book or those you gain from the other sources, you can, of course, earn a decent sum of money as a freelancer.

However, as they say, 'The grass is always greener on the other side.', although you may find the freelancing business quite fascinating when you are an employee and have recently started losing interest in your monotonous lifestyle, the bitter truth is, becoming a freelancer is not as easy as you may think or as it may look from a distance. To be a successful freelancer, it requires a lot of patience, hard work, and a mind open to accept every new concept and knowledge that comes across during your working or nonworking hours.

Well! The question still remains unanswered.

WHY FREELANCING?

There can be several reasons why you may want to become a freelancer rather than continuing with your regular 9-to-5 job that gives you a stable and regular income by the end of every month. Some important factors that may have motivated you to choose freelancing as your career include:

> **Work Environment**
  If you are not good at flattering your seniors and because of this, you are being exploited, demoted, demoralized, humiliated, burdened with unnecessary workload, and

may even get termination threats, you probably have already started looking for other options.

➤ Remuneration

While working for an organization, if you are not paid according to your workload, you would surely get dissatisfied with your current remuneration, and start looking for the alternatives.

➤ Exploitation

If you are ordered to work for additional hours to complete a task with which your employer would earn a decent amount of profit, but you are not paid for your extra time, you feel being exploited. This may ignite your intention to start your own business.

➤ Frequent Switching

If you are a man of dignity and self-respect, and cannot stand unethical behavior from your seniors or colleagues, you are likely to keep switching your jobs quite frequently, thus ending up having a strong inclination towards starting your own business.

➤ Unutilized Skills

If you gained specialization in any field, and your seniors still don't allow you to utilize your skills due to some grievances, you will feel frustrated, and the feeling will increase gradually over time, until you have made up your mind to try your luck in setting up your own business.

➤ No 'Yes Man' Thing

You may have to face hard time as an employee if you are not a 'Yes Man' kind of person who, without questioning anything, agrees to everything that the boss says. "Why don't I start something of my own?" you may ask yourself in such situations.

> ## Pressure Tolerance

If you enjoy your work as long as you are given enough time to complete it, the additional pressure that your employer or seniors may put upon may irritate you, thus encouraging you to finalize the given task inefficiently. This can be yet another motivation for you to start your own business and do the things rightly in your own way.

> ## Exploring

If you don't want to remain stagnant to one domain in the capacity of an office employee you have been doing thus far, you may find the idea of exploring new fields to enhance your area of expertise and skills appealing, and you may further get motivated to start something of your own.

> ## Extra Cash

If you are satisfied with your job and have no intention to switch or quit but still want to earn some extra bucks, you may be interested in working on some projects in your free hours.

Apart from these reasons, there can be several others. It wouldn't be a surprise if you are able to relate your situation with one or more of the above points, and are encouraged to begin your career as a freelancer rather than sticking to your regular 8 hours' job.

However, regardless of the level of enthusiasm you have to become a freelancer, it would be wise to stick to your regular job during your transition period towards your freelancing business. This would save you from the financial crisis that you may face if you quit your job right away. Since it might be challenging to get good business at the initial stage of your freelancing career, your regular job would serve as a backup arrangement for your monthly income.

You can always choose to become a part-time free-lancer while continuing with your regular 9-to-5 job as your primary source of income. You can continue this practice for as long as you want, even forever.

Bypassing Initial Failures

You learn when you succeed, but you learn even more when you fail.

It is generally thought that whenever you try something new, you experience the failures without which there's no way you get success in what you started.

This is not completely true.

Although failures teach you good lessons, why would you seek them when you can avoid them in the first place, and can enjoy the fruits of success right from the first day of your business?

"How is that possible?", you may ask. The answer is, there is no rocket science in this. With merely a few smart actions you can avoid these disheartening and demoralizing failures during the starting phase of your business.

All you need to do is, go through and follow the process given below sincerely.

You fail in doing something due to lack of experience. But what if you gain that experience from others' mistakes? With keen observation and a mind that is always open to learn new things, here's what you can do to avoid the failures even during your first attempts:

➤ **Pick a Target**
  If you are planning to start a new business, look around for a person who has been into the same industry for a while.

> **Background Study**
>
> Check with the background of your target, and assess what mistakes he made during his initial attempts that kept him from succeeding at early stages.

> **Paperwork**
>
> Don't hesitate to do some paperwork. Draw diagrams, use graphs, or try any other such method that can help you better understand the approaches your target made for success, and which among those went wrong.

> **Segregation**
>
> After the proper paperwork, isolate the approaches for failures from those of successes.

> **Analysis**
>
> Deeply analyze the failures of your target along with their possible reasons, and study the success approaches even better.

> **Application**
>
> After proper analysis, you can take your first step toward your business following the approach that helped your target at his early phase.

Feel free to repeat the above procedure on more than one targets for additional case studies. The more cases you study, more accurate your predictions and approaches toward success will be.

In addition to the above procedure, there are a few other tips that you should follow to avoid failures at the initial stage of your business:

> **Slow Pace**

At initial stages, you should work at slow and comfortable pace. Do not hesitate to halt for a while, think about your task, take some time to plan the things, and then start working strategically.

It is better to take the required time to plan things, and then get them done successfully rather than expediting the tasks unnecessarily and ruining everything up, and then starting all over again after experiencing the failure.

> **Feedbacks**

Feedbacks of the projects you completed can be thought of as your result sheet after you have appeared for an examination. Take your feedbacks seriously, and try to strengthen your weak points as indicated in them. Using your feedbacks as weapons to sharpen your skills would surely give you success even at the initial phase of your business.

> **Advices**

Advices from the experienced ones are always valuable to the beginners. It is a good idea to keep taking suggestions from the people who had been in the same situation as you are right now. With such advices and steady speed, you are likely to taste the sweetness of success in your initial attempts.

> **Backup Plan**

Before you start working on any project that has been assigned to you by your client, always consider about the worst case scenario, and prepare a backup plan as how would you handle or completely come out of the situation if something goes wrong.

Having a backup/exit plan doesn't mean that you don't even try to make things right if something bad happens. Rather, you should always give your 100% to complete your assignment successfully, and work even harder to ensure that no such situation arises in future in the first place.

Your backup/exit plan should work as a life-saving jacket that is to be used only when the ship is about to sink and there's no way it can be saved whatsoever.

KEEPING INSPIRATIONS ALIVE

Your inspirations play a vital role in becoming a successful person. You can be inspired by anyone, i.e. a famous celebrity, a genius scientist, a professor of your college, or even by your father, mother or sibling.

It is your inspiration that encourages you to work tirelessly to achieve your goals and move toward your success. Therefore, you should take a picture of the things/people that motivate you, and paste them on the whiteboard or a wall in your room where your focus is likely to fall every time you raise your eyes from your computer screen or papers. If you are motivated with something whose picture you cannot have, write a tagline about it and keep it somewhere in front of your eyes, e.g. your computer's desktop background.

The benefit of this exercise is, each time you get distracted from your work or feel disheartened about your career, the inspirational elements would remind you of your goals and would encourage you to get back to work with full enthusiasm.

In other words, at the time of distraction, the entities related to your inspirations will work as fuel for you, and you'll hear your inner voice telling you, "Hey, you don't have time to waste. If others have already done it, you can do it too. So get back to work and prove your worth to deserve what you desire."

Some other key elements that may come in handy to keep your inspirations alive and healthy include:

> **Motivational Quotes**

Because most of the motivational quotes written by successful people are based on their real-life experiences, reading as many such quotes as possible would keep you from getting disappointed or disheartened, and would further encourage you to continue working until you succeed.

However, in order to get some literal fruits from the quotes, you must try to understand their meaning and make sure to follow them whenever and wherever possible.

> **Success Stories**

Successful people always leave their traces for other to follow.

If you are ambitious, following the footprints of those legends would lead you to your success. All you need to do is, during your initial phase, every time you face hard times, before cursing your life and luck for being cruel to you, use the Internet to search for and go through the success stories of other people. You will be surprised to know that every successful person, without a single exception, was demoralized, rejected, laughed at, or humiliated during his struggling period.

> **Failures**

The Internet search may also redirect you to some pages explaining the life of some personalities who worked hard during their struggling phase but eventually lost their patience and finally withdrew. Reading the stories of such people is equally important because as the lives of successful personalities motivate you to keep trying until you achieve your goals, the life of a person who failed keeps you from giving up.

This is yet another way of ditching the pits without falling into them. No?

> **Observation**

Apart from reading and analyzing the success stories of the famous personalities, another effective way of remaining inspired is to closely observe the successful men around you. Even though such people may not necessarily be world-famous individuals, they can be at much higher scales of their career as compared to the level you are at present. You can observe their dressing sense, body language, their way of communication, etc., and get motivated by the way people appreciate and praise them because of the attributes they possess. Later, you can follow their style to win that kind of appreciation from others for yourself as well.

In short, you can inspire yourself from anything or anyone that you see or meet as long as you have a positive attitude toward your environment you are living in. The point here is, keep in mind that no shortcuts can help you because there aren't any, do your best to remain inspired, and stay determined to achieve what you have planned for.

UNIT 2
SELF PREPARATION

Scope of This Unit

The first thing that you must do before you start something new and different is to prepare yourself. Such kind of preparation includes proper planning, scheduling, and arranging other important things to make your tasks easier, and outputs, better.

This unit focuses on the ethics you should follow and the elements you may need in order to prepare yourself before you roll up your sleeves and get to work.

SIGNIFICANCE OF ATTIRE

This is all about psychology and the games your subconscious and conscious minds play with you.

Although you may find some subheadings under this title irrelevant, by giving them a deeper thought you would surely understand how your dress code helps you in your business in different ways, both directly and indirectly.

As a freelancer, even though you can choose your working hours as per your convenience, starting your day in the morning would be a good idea. Even if you work from home, it is a good practice to take a nice hot shower and wear neat and ironed clothes before you start your day, every day. Where the hot shower freshens your body and gives you mental relaxation, dressing up neatly puts your subconscious mind to 'work mode', which further convinces your conscious mind to act as if you are sitting in an office surrounded by other professionals, thus giving you a virtual corporate environment.

> As a freelancer, and especially when working from home, you don't necessarily have to be in formal cloths i.e. a shirt properly tucked in your trouser, and a tie hanging around your neck. All you need to do is, wear neat, ironed, and comfortable attire so that you can remain active and focused on your assignments during your working hours.

Regardless of your workplace, there are several other benefits of dressing up properly. These advantages can be divided into three main categories namely Direct Benefits, Indirect

Benefits, and Long Term Benefits. All these benefits are explained in detail below:

Direct Benefits

The direct advantages of remaining well-dressed are those that affect your state of mind, personality, and business directly. These benefits are obvious and reflect their results instantaneously. A few such direct benefits include:

➤ **Decorum**

Every work environment has its own decorum that plays an important role in the success of the business. Decent attire reflects good dressing sense which is one of the major factors involved in maintaining proper decorum of the workplace. The same theory applies on you as well even if you are a new freelancer and prefer to work from home.

➤ **Freshness**

Wearing clean, ironed clothes after a hot shower in the morning gives you a fresh feeling. With such freshness right from the moment you start your day, you'll feel energetic and fully motivated, which further enable you to focus on your work in much better way.

➤ **Impression on Clients**

Your decent attire makes you feel more confident while meeting your clients. This confidence presents you as an authentic and reliable professional before them, thus encouraging them to award you with the projects at the prices you demand.

Indirect Benefits

You experience indirect benefits of good dressing sense gradually, i.e. the results are not reflected instantaneously as it is with the direct benefits. A few indirect benefits of good dressing sense are:

> ➤ **Work Efficiency**
>
> With the advantages discussed in the Direct Benefits section, i.e. with proper decorum, fresh and innovative mind, and with self-confidence, your work efficiency improves remarkably. This further enables you to produce better quality output in comparatively lesser time.

> ➤ **Business Growth**
>
> With improved efficiency and the ability to complete your tasks in comparatively lesser time, you can use the additional hours you are left with to work on other projects. This helps you generate more funds that can be used for your business expansion.

Long Term Benefits

In the long run, i.e. when you plan to expand your business, you can carry forward your habit of dressing up nicely while working to set a strong and disciplined foundation for your organization that may have several employees working for you. A few advantages of having good dressing sense in the long run include:

> ➤ **Uniformity**
>
> You can define a uniform for your staff members. This approach is followed by the organizations of repute and helps the employees stay disciplined.

➤ **Branding**

With a proper uniform for your employees, your brand is automatically advertised whenever your staff is on the go, i.e. even while moving from home to office and vice versa.

Even though you may not need to follow all the suggestions given above as they may become applicable only at the certain stages of your business, keeping the benefits of decent attire in mind and following the above suggestions correctly would help you throughout your career.

SCHEDULING WORKDAYS

Proper scheduling of your time is one of the the major key elements of your work efficiency.

Therefore, throughout the globe, all corporates follow the identical work schedule where the employees' 8 hours are divided accordingly to keep them comfortable while working. With such a well-managed and balanced timetable, the employees can start their day properly, have lunch on time, and then finalize the day's task before they leave for home.

On the other hand, although you as a freelancer have the privilege to choose your preferred time to work, it is a good practice to organize even your working hours in a way as if you are following your regular 9-to-5 job schedule. This will keep you mentally active, and, as discussed in the 'Significance of Attire' topic, in 'work mode'.

To elaborate, even if you are new to freelancing and are working from your home, you should follow the proper work schedule as suggested below:

> **Exercise**
  Make sure you exercise daily in order to remain physically fit and active. The pounding heart and open mouth to gasp maximum amount of oxygen in the morning due to the extensive workout would keep you energetic and fresh throughout the day.

> **Heavy Breakfast**
  This is extremely important. Make sure to take heavy breakfast before you start your day. A healthy meal right in the morning will keep you from getting distracted

by the urge of having some snacks every now and then while working.

➤ First-Half

You can start the first-half of your day somewhere between 9:30 AM and 10:00 AM and work till 1:00 PM to 2:00 PM. Since these are the initial hours and your mind is as fresh as new, you can use the time to focus on all the perplexing tasks. If you have some incomplete assignments of the previous day, these would be the right hours to complete them before you start anything new.

> Make sure to take 3 to 5 minutes of rest after every 50 to 60 minutes you work. This would keep your mind relaxed.

➤ Lunch Break

After working for the initial few hours, you can leave your desk for lunch and spend 30 to 45 minutes enjoying your meal and relaxing. If you work from home, you can use this time to lay down and take a nap to relax your brain. You won't find this privilege when you are an employee in an organization.

Note: Make sure not to sleep for too long as it may leave you with the sleepless night that follows, which will further ruin your entire next day due to the disturbed schedule. Setting an alarm during your lunch-time nap would be a wise approach.

➤ Second-Half

After a healthy lunch and probably a snooze, the second-half of the day is to continue with the tasks you were doing in the first-half. A proteinous meal and a nap would make you feel relaxed, thus enabling you to focus with a fresh mind and new energy.

> **Tea Break**

Make sure to take out 5 to 10 minutes for tea break in the evening, i.e. after working for 2 to 3 hours in the second-half. This short recess would keep you from feeling exhausted and tired of working, hence giving you a break from the exertion you might have.

> **Call It a Day**

With a fresh mind after the tea break, it's now time to finalize everything you did throughout the day. Make sure you finish the tasks that are almost at their completion stage, review them, and leave the ones that need more time for the next day. If you have scheduled your time correctly, you won't run out of time while working on a project anyway.

The point is, you should start your day with full enthusiasm, try to complete the previous day's tasks, and work on the mind-boggling stuff during the first-half or maximum by the mid of the second half of your day, i.e. before you leave your table for the tea break. This is because, when you return to your desk after sipping tea or coffee in the evening, somewhere in your mind you know that you are about to call it a day, and because of this, you won't be able to focus much on the work you were doing. Therefore, it would be wise to finalize the things that need less time and attention, and leave the remaining ones for the following day.

The above schedule has been described keeping in mind that you plan to start working in the morning. If you prefer some other time of the day to work, you can organize your time-table accordingly. After all, it's you who will decide at what time you are at your best. Right?

———————

Professional Existence

It's obvious that it takes time and a lot of hard work to get good reviews, become popular, and to take your business to the point where you can generate a decent amount of funds.

As a new freelancer (or even as an old one) you need clients to survive, and in order to get those clients, your professional existence and visibility is must. If you own a website or blog, old or new, or even if you don't, make sure to create your profile on any online freelancers' directory.

Freelancers' online directories are the web portals that contain the databases of both service sellers (freelancers) and buyers (the clients). Since the administrators/owners of the freelancers' directories advertise their site at their ends using the best possible promotional methods, the portals are propagated to the clients all over the world. As the result, the clients keep visiting the portals on a regular basis to look for and hire skilled freelancers. If you have your account there, your profile becomes visible to such clients as well, and if your profile is attractive and all your skills are clearly mentioned in there, your chances of being awarded with the projects increase.

To create an account and decorate your profile on any freelancers' directory, the following elements play a vital role:

> **Account Creation**
> Of course, you must have an account in order to avail the facilities that the freelancers' directories have to offer. Make sure you use your original name and provide the other required details correctly.

➤ **Profile Picture**

In addition to creating your account, it is also important to decorate your profile. One of the major objects that attract the potential clients and enable them to identify your profile at a single glance is your display picture a.k.a. profile picture. Make sure you set an attractive and unique picture your profile page. The recommendation is, use your original photo in order to make it easy for others to recognize you.

➤ **Your Expertise**

Make sure you mention your area of specialization in detail along with the experience you have gained in that field till date. If possible, provide the links where your work can be seen in function. This would help your clients assess the efficiency of your work and your authenticity.

➤ **Other Skills**

In addition to having specialization in one field, you may also have decent knowledge in other domains. For example, if you are an IT professional, along with gaining expertise in PHP programming, you may also be good in databases, Visual Basic, or even animations. Make sure to mention such skills to your profile as well along with your exposure till date in those areas.

➤ **Availability of Time**

With your profile on an online freelancers' directory, you are likely to be contacted by the clients from all over the world, including those who belong to different time zones. To avoid any kind of misunderstanding, make sure to mention your time zone and your availability hours, i.e. the time when you are available for communication and your clients can expect your replies/responses.

➤ **Website/Blog Info (If Any)**

If you don't have your website or a blog, it is recommended to get one. If you want to avoid any initial investments in purchasing a domain and getting your website built, there are many online portals that offer blogging services for free. As a new freelancer, you can use any of these sites to create your own blog, and can go for a website of your own once you start earning.

While creating your website/blog, make sure that it contains your detailed information, links or demos of your previous works, and the reviews your clients gave you for your projects. After populating your blog/site with your detailed information, create its backlink in your freelancers' profile.

➤ **Backlinks**

It is strongly suggested to provide a backlink to your own website or blog when creating your profile on any such portal. Backlinks are the URLs that you place on your freelancers' portal's profile. These backlinks, when clicked, redirect your profile viewers to your website or blog. This helps in increasing the traffic to your page, thus making the visitors aware of your professional existence. This, of course, further helps you generate more business.

In addition to populating your profile with the above mentioned important information, it is also necessary to explore and use other features offered by such portals to get the best out of them. Such features may include:

➤ **Bidding**

When clients post their projects on such freelancing sites along with the estimated price they are willing to pay, you as a freelancer can place your bids on them. Many sites allow the freelancers to place bids for free but deduct some service fee for each project that is awarded to them.

➤ **Managing Projects**

On such portals, you can also manage the projects you have been awarded so far. With the tools available on the sites, you can:

- → Mark projects as complete
- → Mark projects as delayed
- → Mark projects as 'in progress'
- → Request for payments
- → Prioritize the projects
- → Set deadlines for each project

There can be many other tools available on the sites that can help you work more efficiently in lesser time.

➤ **Managing Team**

In addition to managing your projects, you can also create a team and organize and manage its members for better output. For example, you can:

- → Add team members
- → Remove members
- → Assign projects to your team
- → Distribute sections/modules among your team members

With the team management tools, you can easily manage your personnel while keeping an accurate and most updated track of the progress of your projects at the same time.

➤ **Invoicing**

The freelancers' directories also allow you to generate different types of invoices and send them to your clients. Many portals even enable you to create invoices for partial payments.

Free and Paid Features

Almost every online freelancers' directory offers many of its features for free to be used by the freelancers. Once your clientele is increased and you add more members to your team, by paying a nominal amount you can upgrade your subscription to the premium plan that offers many advanced features that allow you to manage your clients and team more easily and efficiently.

Note: Not all freelancers' directories offer all the features discussed above. Some may have most of the tools available for you, while others may remain limited to a few ones only. At some instances, you may even need to sign up on multiple portals for team/client management and bidding on projects. Nonetheless, most of these services are free anyway.

It is as important to manage your clients and team efficiently as it is to decorate your profile on any freelancers' directory. Where a nicely decorated profile attracts new potential clients to take a look at it, the ability to manage your clientele and team efficiently reflects your professionalism toward your work.

At any point of time, if you feel that things are getting hard to manage, you can upgrade your plan to avail premium services offered by the portal you have signed up with, and exploit the advanced features to manage your stuff more smoothly.

BEING THE BEST

Doing something is one thing but being the best in what you do is entirely a different story altogether.

Regardless of the field of your work, make sure you do your job the correct way and that no one else is better than you, at least not in the nearby areas. That being said, to become successful, you don't have to be a jack of all trades. All you need is, get specialization in any one of the fields of your interest, and work hard to gain excellence in it.

Although it is a well-known fact that you cannot master anything, especially when talking about technology, you must make sure that you are knowledgeable enough to present yourself as a better alternative among your competitors when bidding for the new projects.

A few tips on excelling in your field include:

> **Read**

Read as much as you can. This is something you must always do. Even if you are tired, reading something related to your work for at least 15 minutes before you sleep helps you increase your knowledgebase and awareness consistently. With regular reading and implementing your new information in your work, you gradually upgrade yourself to the next level of your expertise.

> **Practice**

When you are new to freelancing, there might be instances where you won't have any projects to work on. Even in such situations, it is advisable that you think of some project of your own begin working on it. For example, if you are into animations and don't have any assignment to work on, think of a new, creative and challenging project and proceed with it, until you are awarded with a project from a client. This will keep you in practice and the challenges in the project would help you improve your skills. After you are awarded with an assignment, you can halt your own project, and begin with the awarded one.

➤ Betterment

No matter how good your finished project is, there is always some room for improvement. Therefore, after you believe that you have completed your assignment, review the output thoroughly, and make any changes to it that you find necessary. However, make sure not to review the project more than twice as doing so may lead you to a confused state of mind, and eventually, you may unintentionally degrade the quality of your work.

➤ Social Network Community

You cannot expect to be perfect in your work until you share your ideas with others and are ready to accept theirs in return. Building a social network of like-minded people, especially from the same profession, and communicating with them on the matters of your interest as often as possible would be a wise way to improve and gain excel in your skills.

➤ Personal Library

As it is said, 'A person with a book is never alone.'. Since reading plays a vital role in your progress, it is strongly suggested that you maintain your personal library at your office or home or both, and populate it with as many reference books and other informative material related to your area of specialization as you possibly can. It is also important to add new books to your library regularly in order to remain updated in your field.

You can expect projects from your existing and new clients only when you are good at your work and have previous records of successfully completed assignments to justify your proficiency. If you want to maintain a long-term relationship with your clients, you must specialize and gain excel in your field. Using the proven records of the prior projects and your level of knowledge and experience, you must assure your clients that it is only you, and no one else, who can do the given assignment with accuracy and efficiency.

For instance, if you are a freelancer blogger who writes on latest technologies and gadgets, you must read as much as possible to become more proficient in creating engaging texts, and keep yourself updated with the latest trends/technologies as well. Doing so will encourage the quality-conscious clients to hire you every time they need some assignments to be completed. Of course there would be many others to compete you, but if you have an indifferent way of presenting yourself and some quality-reflecting samples to demonstrate, you will surely win the race.

If you are new to the business and do not have any sample work to demonstrate, try making some of your own. For example, if you deal in tangible products, use the free online stores to place the pictures of the produced goods. Likewise, if you are into services, you can use the free online forums or blogging sites to explain the visitors/clients what do you do and how you do it.

Although it is recommended that you get your own domain and web hosting, which can be purchased at extremely cheap rates these days, as a startup if you do not wish to invest funds, picking the free alternatives available online would be a good start.

UNIT 3
IMPROVEMENTS &
UPGRADES

Scope of This Unit

When you start working, you improve, and those improvements help you grow. In other words, regular improvements in your work, behavior, skills, and efficiency are the key elements to your success.

This unit covers in detail how you can improve and upgrade yourself to become a better and more skilled person than you are today.

IMPROVEMENTS

Even the stagnant water gets infected and causes serious diseases.

Regular advancements are mandatory to keep up with the world, and if you are into business, continuous improvements in your skills and products are the key elements to your success.

As it is with other things, there's a certain process to improving yourself or the services/goods you deal in. Therefore, it is important to learn the correct method to be a better person than you are now, and to get a successful career.

Also, before going any further, you must understand that there's no threshold to begin or quit self or career improvements. In other words, regardless of your position, stage, status, or level of success you are at, there's always more room for betterment, and all you need is, an open and egoless mind to realize the fact that there is a lot more to learn and improve other than you currently know and have.

Key Points for Improvement

Below are the key points that you must follow in the correct order to ensure your proper improvements without any adverse effects.

The points can be segregated in two categories. Where the first category consists of the process of improving yourself as an individual, the second category explains in what ways you can use the first category to get a successful career.

Self-Improvement

➤ Observation

You learn when you observe things carefully. Start observing the successful people around you during social and/or official gatherings. While observing them, notice their dressing sense, style, way of talking, and how they carry and present themselves. If possible, go ahead and talk to them for a minute or two. The point here is, the deeper and closer your observation is, the easier would it be for you to follow.

➤ Application

Once you have deeply observed your target, start applying the observed attributes in your behavior and see how others react to your changed nature. Don't worry if no one notices you initially. Continue with the application and in no time you will be a different personality altogether.

➤ Improvement

In any situation, learn from your mistakes or failures and start improving yourself instead of getting disheartened or demoralized. At this point, try to think what other successful people (including the one you observed) would do if they were in the same situation as you are.

Even if you fail, keep calm, try to understand the reason of the failure, and once found, keep it in mind as a good lesson, and never repeat the mistake.

Career/Business Improvements

You can follow the Observation, Application, and Improvement points in the Self-Improvement category in the correct order to improve the following aspects of your business:

> **Management**

  If you've not been doing this so far, use the three points in the Self-Improvement category to learn and follow how to keep everything (such as your account books, client and project records, files, and other important data) well-organized from now and onward. This will help you manage things easily when expanding your business to become a medium-scale and then a large-scale organization.

> **Expansion**

  Use the steps given in the first category to learn how to and then start thinking about business expansion right from today itself. Make sure to set your short term goal or the first milestone where you would like to see yourself a year from now, and work hard accordingly. Once you reach the first milestone, use the same procedure to set and achieve the second, and then the third, fourth, fifth and more milestones that you set thereafter.

It would be good if you pick one successful person at a time as your target, and apply the three points from the first category on him. If your target runs a business, apply the remaining two points from the second category on him as well. Once you think you have learned enough and there's nothing more to extract from your target, pick a different person and start over.

Repeat this process with as many people and for as long as you can. The more you practice, the better you become.

You can learn anything from anyone at any time. Although out of ignorance, sometimes even the kids say something that is of great importance. Therefore, keep your ears, eyes, and mind open to accept new things from the ordinary people as well, and use the new information for your and your business' improvement.

UPGRADES

This title may sound redundant to the previous one but there is a different between improving yourself and upgrading.

Improvement involves polishing your entities and attributes such as renovating your workplace or gaining excel in a technology. On the other hand, upgrading yourself means you are going for a different, rather better version of a stuff altogether. For example, if you are getting proficient in one technology on a regular basis, that would be your improvement, whereas learning a new technology is your upgradation.

Both upgradation and improvement are important for your business and career. This is because, if you stop learning, you will end up having obsolete knowledge which most of your clients won't appreciate much. Therefore, as a business person, in addition to improving yourself, it is also mandatory to keep upgrading your knowledgebase, technical or non-technical skills, and working style in order to keep up with today's competitive market. With the upgraded and up-to-date information, you can communicate with your clients more confidently, and can easily convince them to award you with the projects.

Another advantage of regularly upgrading yourself is, your work efficiency and productivity automatically improves, thus giving you more positive feedbacks from your clients.

A wise approach would be to subscribe for the relevant newsletters, social media pages, and informational websites, and regularly download the meaty information that would help you upgrade your skills and expand your business. You can also become member of a few renowned online libraries from where you can read the relevant books online, or can borrow/purchase a softcopy of the material with ease.

Another Aspect of Upgrading

Upgrading yourself does not always and only involve gaining knowledge or deeply indulging yourself in studies or labs. Instead, along with all these, you must also upgrade your:

> **Dressing Sense**

It is your communication that makes you impressive alright, but what encourages people to involve in communication with you in the first place? It is your wardrobe.

If you are not nicely dressed up, people won't notice you or may even hesitate interacting with you. Therefore, make sure to keep up with the latest fashion trends, and whenever possible, wear branded clothes, especially in public gatherings or parties, or the places where you expect to meet potential clients face-to-face.

> **Gadgets and Other Wearables**

Even the gadgets are the part of your wearables these days, and therefore upgrading to the latest ones whenever possible would be a wise idea. A few examples can be:

→ The latest model of your smartphone adds status to your personality.

→ If you are a techie, a tablet or advanced laptop would justify your profession.

→ A branded wristwatch would reflect your royal living sense.

➤ Lifestyle

Upgrading to a good and healthy lifestyle is yet another way of reflecting your class. For example:

→ Make sure to pick a decent restaurant every time you are among your friends or with friends of friends.

→ Have nutritious meals.

→ If using public transportation, whenever possible, avoid using a shared vehicle such as a public bus. Rent a taxi instead, especially when with others or while going for a party.

➤ Physical Fitness

Looking good is as important as wearing branded clothes and carrying latest gadgets. In order to live a healthy lifestyle, make sure you are and remain physically fit. As discussed earlier, you must exercise daily to remain toned and in good shape. This would make you feel more confident, and more importantly, you'll look good in any dress you wear.

➤ Personal Vehicle

Many times you are being judged by the vehicle you drive. Where an old and dusty private transportation medium of yours reflects your careless nature, a new and rather clean vehicle shows your taste about lifestyle. That being said, whenever possible, make sure to change your vehicle to an upper version that would help you feel more confident and look more trendy.

> If you can't buy a new vehicle, make sure to keep your existing one neat, timely serviced, and in good condition.

The above list is for your reference, only to give you an idea as how and in what ways you can upgrade yourself. You can take your time, think well, and can add as many points to the list as you can come up with as per your convenience. Don't worry if you aren't able to follow every point given above. Things do take time, but they happen if you are determined.

The bottom-line is, you can't think of becoming a business tycoon while staying still and sitting idle. In order to achieve your goals, regular efforts and, although at slow pace, continuous improvements and upgrades are crucial.

UNIT 4
OFFICE PREPARATION

Scope of This Unit

Once you have decided to become a freelancer, you need a place to work from. However, before you start using an area as your workplace, you must decorate it properly to give it a look of an office. This will give you an official environment while working, thus allowing you to focus on your tasks.

This unit describes the ways to convert a normal room into a full-fledged workplace from where you can begin your journey toward your success.

Sitting Postures

Peaceful mental state enables your brain to work preperly, efficiently, and at full.

In any work environment, your sitting posture affects your mental state, and further, the quality of your work. Once you have decided to start your career as a freelancer, the first thing that you must do is to understand the significance of comfortable sitting, and arrange and place its components accordingly.

At the initial phase of your freelancing business, you are not expected to have a team of several professionals working under you, and you are likely to work alone, probably from your home. Considering this, the primary factor that would impact the comfort of your sitting is an isolated workplace. Any separate room within your residence (if you plan to work from home) where you can work for 8 to 10 hours every day without any disturbance should serve the purpose well.

After you manage to get a separate room for your work, it is now time to think about using its space optimally by equipping it with the ingredients that would play a vital role in giving you proper sitting posture and comfort. These components are:

Ingredients of Comfortable Sitting

> **A Comfortable Chair**
> A comfortable chair is important as you will be spending a lot of time on it. A nicely designed chair stuffed with good quality foam allows you to work on your desk for long hours, thus encouraging you to give more con-

centration and time to your assignments without getting bored or exhausted. This further helps you produce quality output, and earn decent feedbacks and good remunerations that follow as the outcome of your efficient work.

Some important parts and features that make a chair comfortable include:

- → Armrest
- → Long backrest
- → Lumbar back support
- → Wheels
- → Revolving system
- → Hydraulic height adjustment system
- → Adjustable backrest

Buying a large size executive chair (the one that big bosses have) would be a good idea. Since such chairs have almost all the above mentioned features and parts, you can relax on them when tired.

> **A Big Table**

Your table should be big enough to hold all your necessary stationary items, and mission-critical devices and gadgets such as:

- → Your desktop/laptop computer
- → Your cellphone(s)
- → Your important papers and files
- → Other daily use stationeries such as a pen stand, paperweights, table calendar, etc.

In addition to the above, your table should also have:

→ A proper footrest to allow your knees to bend at the correct angle, thus giving you a comfortable sitting posture.

→ A few drawers with built-in lock system to safely keep your important papers and objects like:
  ➤ Accounts maintenance files
  ➤ Phone and electricity bills
  ➤ Clients' records and their invoicing details
  ➤ Business cards (if any)
  ➤ Pack of blank DVDs
  ➤ USB drives
  ➤ Computer's driver installation discs, etc.

By keeping all the important things mentioned above within your arm's reach on a big table, you can complete your tasks comparatively sooner and without getting tired. Also, a large size table would give you spacious area that you can use to work more freely and efficiently to produce quality output.

➤ **A Decent Air Conditioning System**

Although indirectly linked, a decent air conditioning system is also an important component when counting the ingredients of a good and comfortable sitting. No matter how soft your executive chair or big your table is, a proper air conditioning system is essential to maintain pleasant room temperature so that you can focus on your work and produce quality output without getting distracted due to the unfriendly weather.

> Even though it is likely that you already have a good air conditioning system in your room, if you don't, investing a few hundred bucks to get one for yourself would be a wise approach.

Arranging the Ingredients

Once you manage to get everything discussed above, your next move should be to place things in a proper way so that you can extract the most out of them. A few tips that can help you in this context include:

> ➤ **Table Placement (In Accordance with Air Conditioning System)**
>
> Place the table at a proper distance from the air conditioning system. Keeping it too close to the vent where the air can hit your face directly with force while working may give you headache after sometime. Likewise, picking a distant area from the air vent to place the table would make you feel uncomfortable during unfriendly weather.
>
> When choosing a perfect place for your table, you may need to calculate the area where your chair would go in accordance with it, and where your face would be while using your computer or when working on papers. Since you cannot move your table too frequently, make sure that your calculations are as accurate as possible.

> ➤ **Chair Placement (In Accordance with Table)**
>
> After this, take your time to calculate and place your chair at an appropriate distance from the table.
>
> Since it is the chair that you will be sitting on (probably

for long durations), this calculation is important to ensure that you can work comfortably for 8 to 10 hours.

Depending on the weather of your region and how your body reacts to it, maintaining appropriate distance between your body and the air vent of the air conditioning system would help you work for long hours without losing your efficiency.

It is more important to arrange the furniture properly than considering its quality when buying it. Where the wrongly aligned good quality furniture may give you hard times while working, average quality chair, table, and air conditioning system can remarkably increase your work efficiency when placed correctly.

Although often taken too lightly, the ease of recycling the waste products is also an important part of your comfortable sitting. The trashcan should either be close to either of your legs under the table, or at the corner that is nearest to your chair in the room. This will ensure that you don't have to stress yourself when recycling something, and it can be done without any hassle.

To sum up, do not hesitate to invest a small amount of money to buy yourself some decent furniture that can add comforts to your sitting arrangement as doing so will help you work efficiently and produce quality output. Also, take your time to assess the correct location for each of the components involved in your comfortable sitting to ensure that you use the furniture in the best possible way.

ALIGNING OBJECTS

In this digital age, you are likely to do most of your work on a computer.

Because of this, when working as a freelancer, you must consider your desktop or laptop PC one of the most important mission-critical entities for your business, and you must make sure that it is placed on your desk at the right position where you can continue using it for hours without getting tired or losing your work efficiency.

Depending on the type of computer you are using, i.e. a desktop or laptop, its placement may vary. Also, following are some other factors that also play important role when placing your computer correctly on your desk:

> Height of your table
> Height of your chair
> Distance between your table and chair
> Height of the upper portion of your body
> Length of your arms
> Your eyesight

Considering the above factors, the best way to correctly align your desktop or laptop computer on your work table would be:

> **When Using a Laptop PC**

If you are using a laptop, you should consider placing it on the table in such a position that while using its keyboard, at least half of your arms (up to 6 inches of your arms starting from your wrists) below the elbows are resting on the table. This will ensure that you can use the keyboard and touchpad to type and navigate respectively without feeling any pressure or pain on your arms and fingers. Also, because of the proper distance between your eyes and the laptop screen, your eyes won't feel any strain when working for long hours.

➤ When Using a Desktop Computer

In case you have a desktop computer, make sure that:

➔ You place its keyboard on the table in such a way that at least half of your arms (up to 6 inches of your arms starting from your wrists) below the elbows are properly resting on the table while you type.

➔ The mouse is placed right beside the keyboard, i.e. parallel to it.

➔ The monitor is at a comfortable, and most importantly, safe distance so that your eyes feel no strain.
Note: Using an LED monitor would be a good idea.

➔ The system case, a.k.a. CPU in general terms, is kept somewhere below the table and not on it.

➔ The complete computer system is connected to a good quality UPS (Uninterrupted Power Supply) in order to avoid any accidental data loss or file corruption.

Since it is a desktop PC and has its peripherals such as keyboard, mouse, and monitor separately connected to it, the above alignment suggestions must be followed correctly in order to ensure that you can work without getting exhausted or putting your eyesight at risk.

In addition to your computer system, the other mission-critical objects for your business are your chair and table, and their well-calculated and correct alignment is essential to make the necessary stationary items and important documents easily accessible to you, while keeping your sitting posture comfortable. Therefore, you should make sure that everything is in proper order and place so that you can work with comfort and peace of mind, and have everything within your arm's reach.

Below are a few suggestions that may be helpful in this context:

➤ **Chair Alignment**

Your chair should be aligned with your table and the computer kept on it properly to make sure you can sit straight while your back is resting at its backrest, and that your feet can comfortably rest on the footrest under the table when you are working. The type of chair explained in the previous title would be a good purchase.

➤ **Ease of Accessibility**

Your table and chair should be aligned with each other in such a way that other stationaries and objects such as important files, notepads, paperweights, business cards, etc. remain within your arms' reach, and you don't have to stretch your body extensively in order to grab any stuff when needed.

With these arrangements, regardless of your sitting position, you will feel comfortable when working for long hours or doing some real brainstorming, without getting physically or mentally exhausted.

Spicing Your Office

A colorful environment of your office is always productive as compared to monochrome walls and pre-historic termites-eaten furniture.

Even if you are efficient and work hard for long hours throughout the day, a colorless office cannot encourage you to produce quality-enriched output whatsoever. On the other hand, a decorated and fragranced environment gives a peaceful mental state and makes you more productive, efficient in your work, and also enables you to focus on your tasks in a better way.

When it comes to improving your workplace's ambiance, the entire process can be completed in three steps that are explained in detail below:

➤ **Office Decoration**

Since it is your office, it's you who needs to take care of it and make sure that it looks good. This step requires you to take initiative to decorate your office with the best possible items. A few things that can help you in this include:

➜ **Eco-Friendly Objects**

In addition to getting good furniture for your office to make your sitting comfortable, add some plants or flowerpots or both to your workplace as well. Also, make sure to put fresh flowers in the flowerpot regularly. These items not only decorate your office but also make the environment fresh and live.

➔ **Wall Decoration**

Beautifying the walls of your workplace is also an important part of office decoration. You can put some color paintings on the walls to make them look beautiful. Pasting some posters with motivational quotes on the walls is yet another good idea. If you want, you can add both paintings and motivational posters in combination to make your workplace look more professional.

Note: Make sure not to add too many items to the wall as doing so may make the room congested.

➢ **Office Aroma**

It is as important that your office smells good as it is to decorate it with eco-friendly and other decorative items. Breathing in fresh and scented air relaxes your mind and releases your stress. A few suggestions that may help you in this can be:

➔ **Air Fresheners**

Using an air freshener multiple times a day keeps the environment and ambience of your office fresh and pleasant. Since the air fresheners come in variety of fragrances to choose from, it is advisable to switch to different flavors from time to time in order to avoid monotonous aroma of your office.

➔ **Incense Sticks**

Since the joss sticks are mostly used in religious and spiritual ceremonies, it is a good idea to start your day by using one at your workplace. Doing so won't only add natural fragrance to your office, it would also give a divine ambiance to the room.

➤ Office Cleanliness

Note: Although this topic is explained in detail in the next title, briefly discussing it here would be good for introductory, consistency, and contextual purposes.

An eco-friendly office with pleasant fragrance won't do any good if it is dirty. Therefore, it is extremely important to keep your workplace neat and tidy. This can be done by:

→ Regular Dusting

Regular dusting of your workplace gives it a new freshness every day. You can use an old piece of cloth to wipe the dust off your furniture and other decorative items. You should follow this practice at least once on alternate days, if not daily. If possible, you can use a portable vacuum cleaner for dusting.

→ Furniture Maintenance

In addition to dusting your furniture regularly, polishing them from time to time is another way of ensuring its long life. Make sure to polish your furniture at least once in a year so that it remains as good as new and serves you well.

Apart from you taking initiatives to maintain your office decorum and its decoration, you must also educate your staff members (if you happen to hire some) to:

→ Keep Their Desks Tidy

Policy of tidiness results in hygienic ambiance of

your workplace in the long run. Make sure that everyone throughout your office follows it.

→ **Wear Light and Decent Perfume/Deodorant**

Smart and clean staff members are the key elements for maintaining decorum and decent environment in every office. Make sure to ask your employees to wear tidy dress and decent perfume/deodorant while coming to the office every day.

A few other tips which, when followed make your workplace look up-to-date and lively are:

➤ **Dates**

Write the current date on the whiteboard daily. This will give you a psychological impact of keeping yourself update, and will also reflect your activeness and passion toward your work to your office visitors.

➤ **Celebrations**

Always decorate your office and invite your allies and friends on celebrations likes Thanksgiving, Christmas, and New Year Night. This will ensure that you remain in touch with your social circle, and maintain a healthy personal and professional relationship with them.

With all the above tips correctly followed, you can make your work area (even if it is a single room) look lively and have healthy environment. Having such atmosphere in your office will encourage you to produce quality work, and will also motivate your staff members to stay active and work smartly.

Do not hesitate to do the above activities on your own if you can't hire a dedicated person to help you at the initial stage of your career. Always remember, the habits you make (good or bad) at your earlier freelancing age will play vital role in carving your professional career in the long run.

CLEANING WORKPLACE

Neat and tidy work area brings positive vibes.

Also, a clean and well-arranged work area (even if it a small room in your home) reflects your efficient management and gives you an encouraging ambiance to work.

Keeping your workplace clean is not as hectic or troublesome task as it may seem. Generally, if you have a single room in the beginning of your career, you can use a small piece of cloth for daily dusting. Apart from this, the alternate options you have include:

> **Helper**

Although in many regions of the world the helpers are not cheap, if you can afford or if you live in the country where such labors are easily available at low cost, hiring one for dusting purposes would be a wise approach. Doing so won't only save your energy and time but will also give you a clean ambiance right from the moment you enter your office. This wouldn't be possible if you plan to do all the dusting on your own.

> **Vacuum Cleaner**

It is not expensive, and the chances are that you already have one at your place. If not, a good quality vacuum cleaner won't cost you more than $100. This option can be chosen if you don't want to hire a helper and want to do all the dusting yourself while making your task as easy and quick as possible at the same time. With a vacuum cleaner, all the dusting of your workplace can be done within a few minutes, without giving you any physical overhead.

Once you have decided which option would you prefer to maintain cleanliness in your office, you must consider dusting the following things regularly to keep them clean and tidy:

➤ **Your Desktop or Laptop PC**

Since your computer is one of the mission-critical entities for your business, make sure to keep its keyboard, mouse (or touchpad in case of laptop), monitor, and system case a.k.a. CPU (in case of desktop) clean by wiping off the dust from it on a regular basis. Keeping these items dust free will ensure their long lives and smooth performance, hence giving you a hinder-free user-experience.

➤ **Your Furniture**

Dusting your office furniture daily gives you a hygienic environment that keeps you at peaceful mental state and gradually increases your work efficiency. Therefore, this is as important as it is to keep your computer dust-free and fully updated with latest anti-virus applications and other security programs.

➤ **Your Files and Other Papers**

Tidiness also includes keeping your daily-use papers and files properly organized. Keep all your paperwork like physical records of your purchases, phonebook, documentations, etc. properly arranged. If possible, get a bookshelf, place all the files and papers in it in the categorized way, and label the sections of the shelf accordingly. This way you can easily find your stuff when needed.

> ## Floor and Walls of Your Room

It is also important to mop the floor of your workplace regularly, and use a piece of cloth or vacuum cleaner on the walls once in a week or fortnightly. This will keep them free from dust or other stains that may make your work area look messy.

> ## Your Dustbin

Sounds strange? Fair enough. But look at the other side. Even though your dustbin is there to hold all your trash, you can't leave the wastes in there forever. Emptying your dustbin daily or on alternate days gives your mind a feel of fresh start.

Another Aspect of Cleanliness

Cleanliness doesn't only consist of mopping your floor, cleaning the walls of the room, or dusting your furniture and computer. It also includes cleaning the non-tangible mission-critical objects of your business. One such example can be:

> ## Desktop Window

A messy and overcrowded desktop window of your PC would impede the process of locating the needed files or folders. Also, if the hard drive of your computer has several unnecessary files in it, the PC's performance may decrease.

That being said, along with cleaning your computer physically, running any free or paid PC optimization tool and removing any unwanted files or folders from it would remarkably improve its working, thus giving you a flawless end-user experience.

In all, a clean and well-maintained work area and the mission-critical objects such as your devices, stationary, documents, etc. increase your work efficiency, thus helping you become more productive and deliver quality output.

———————

No App Purchases

Free is always good. Right? ;)

Being at the initial stage of your journey toward becoming a successful freelancer, it is not expected from you to invest a lot of money in purchasing expensive stuff unless you have unlimited funds to spend.

That being said, since you are likely to do most of your tasks on a computer, in the beginning of your freelancing business, you should download and use the free applications that are required to complete your projects. Except for the interface which may differ from their paid alternatives, generally, such free programs offer almost identical features, thus allowing you to work on the given assignments without any issues.

A few examples to explain this clearly can be:

➤ **Example 01**

If you are into content creation, and need a text editor to work on, you do not have to purchase an expensive package right away. Instead, you can go for any of its free substitutes such as Apache OpenOffice or LibreOffice and can use it to write the articles/blogs for your clients.

➤ **Example 02**

If you are into application development, you will find many free tools that would allow you to type your codes with ease, and produce the identical outputs as any other paid application could come up with.

Some free but useful development tools include:

- ➜ CoffeeCup Free HTML Editor
- ➜ Notepad++
- ➜ Firebug
- ➜ PageBreeze
- ➜ WebMatrix
- ➜ MySQL, etc.

In addition to the above, a quick online search would show you several links to other open source development tools for your preferred platform. All you need to do is, download the tools, understand how they work, and start working on them to develop the programs.

Using open source (free) applications is a smart approach that every freelancer, including you must take at the initial level. After being a freelancer for a while and moving toward a successful career, once you have saved enough funds to afford sophisticated paid applications to expedite your work process, you can invest your earnings in buying them. Doing so would not only ease your work but would also make your work process look more advanced and professional.

However, the idea still remains the same. Even after becoming a successful freelancer, and further, an entrepreneur, you would still like to spend as less money as possible and extract the most out of the free resources to gain the maximum possible benefit from them. Won't you?

Many people use the free tools even at the advanced stages of their career as well unless there is a precise need to buy the paid program, or the paid alternative has any particular feature that is not available in the free tool they use.

UNIT 5
BUSINESS PREPARATION

Scope of This Unit

After motivating and preparing yourself, and setting up your office, you are now ready to do business.

But wait!

Where's the business plan? Of course you are a freelancer but even that business needs some preparation.

This unit explains which key elements you must focus on to prepare and start with your freelancing business.

Planning the Business

A proper and strictly followed business strategy can bring success to you before you even know.

Same is the case with freelancing. To become a successful freelancer and earn a decent sum of money, it is important to plan your entire strategy right from the start, i.e. before you even begin working.

In addition to planning, there are a few other phases that you must go through to become a successful freelancer and further, an ideal businessperson. In fact, it is a complete cycle which, when followed correctly gives you the career you've dreamed of.

The cycle of becoming a successful freelancer consists of the following phases:

➤ **Planning**

Since planning is the initial step toward your bright career, it demands days, or sometimes even months of brainstorming. A few tips that can help you plan your business strategy correctly are:

➜ **Start with Paperwork**

Note down all your streams of work where you have good hands-on. For example, if you are good at programming, note down all the languages that you are well-versed with. Likewise, if you are good at graphics designing, mention on the paper all the tools that you can use to create good graphics, designs, and models.

→ **Prioritization**

After listing your work areas, prioritize the entries in the list according to your expertise level, i.e. beginner, intermediate, or moderate. This will help you bid on the correct projects and enable you to produce quality output.

→ **Market Research and Costing**

Your next step should be to check with the other freelancers (your competitors) in your area or online, i.e. from where you intend to pitch your services to the clients. Have a close look at what they are doing and at what prices.

→ **Define a Price List**

Using the results of your research, set the prices at which you wish to offer your services to your clients. A professional approach would be to set standard prices for your services, and give the same rates to all the clients while bidding on the projects.

➤ **Implementation**

Once you are through with the planning stage, roll up your sleeves and start acting upon your idea. Make sure to follow your strategy exactly the way you planned. This will help you bring your ideas to the real world comparatively quickly, thus helping you become a successful freelancer in a short while.

➤ **Improvements**

You may face hard times and even some downfalls during the initial phase of your freelancing business. When this happens, instead of getting disheartened or demoralized, remain open to inhale new ideas, take the failures as lessons, and use them as your tools to sharpen your skills to produce improved quality output in your future projects.

> **Expansion**

Once you have made remarkable improvements up to the level where you are considered proficient in your line of work, it is now time to move further and explore other areas to work on. While doing so, you can again follow the same cycle of Planning→Implementation →Improvements→Expansion but with the new field of work this time.

You can repeat the above cycle for as many new areas and as many times as you wish. The only difference while following the cycle from the second time and onward would be, you will be already motivated and have enough resources and funds to support your expansion process.

Although going through the cycle of the business phases requires a lot of effort, you need to be patient and should analyze the outcomes of each phase carefully as you cover them. You should also think about the failures, and prepare some backup plan to overcome them with least efforts and minimum time.

Moving forward in a planned way saves you a decent amount of time. This also makes you strong and confident enough to face the obstructions whenever they try to block or hinder your journey toward your success.

Significance of Logo

A single picture is more explanatory than the 1000 words when it comes to describing something.

Likewise, it doesn't matter much what the name of your site or blog, or the URL of your domain is. An attractive graphical symbol that can represent your business, and can help others to quickly point out your blog/website/services/products among several others is something you need in every phase of your career.

This is where a professionally created logo comes into the picture.

Some obvious advantages of having a business logo can be:

> **Professional Face**
> A unique and attractive logo doesn't only give your business (even as a freelancer) a professional look but it also works as a face for you or your organization. When a decent logo is propagated well, you no longer need to use your full name or the name of your business for advertisement or communication, as the picture says it all.

> **Authenticity**
> With a good logo, your new (or even old) clients can know that you are a brand, are authentic, and can be trusted. This further makes them feel that their projects are in the hands of a professional.

> **Scalability**
> Since you look authentic with the presence of a business logo, it becomes easier for you to hire skilled staff to as-

sist you in your projects whenever needed. The indirect benefit for this would be, with more helping hands, you can work on more projects simultaneously, hence covering more assignments every month and earning more funds.

> **Build Trust**
  While making business contracts/deals with your clients and allies, a professional looking logo printed on your business card makes you look more trustworthy and reliable.

How to Get a Logo?

If you are an IT person, you may be aware of some of the most commonly used image creating and editing tools such as Adobe Photoshop, CorelDRAW, GIMP, etc., and most likely you already have a basic understanding of any of these applications as how to use them to design a good logo. However, if you are not from computer background or don't know how to create your own logo, the following options can help you get one for your business:

> **Using Image Creating Tools**
  Because it is only you who understands your business and area of work well, no one can visualize the face of your business logo better than you. With any of the paid or free image creation tools, you can put your imagination on to the computer screen, and further get it printed on your business card and published on your blog or website.

  A brief online search can give you a list of several image editing tools to choose from. You can pick the one that best fits your needs and has a user-friendly interface as well.

➤ Using Online Logo Makers

If you don't want to use any image creating tool, using the online logo makers would be a good idea. Many online logo making sites allow you to create a business logo for free. Also, at nominal prices, these websites offer premium services that you can subscribe for in order to use their advanced tools and get assistance from the professionals they have.

➤ Hire a Professional

If you are not much of a DIY person, hiring a professional from your local area would be your best bet. Although doing so would cost you some money, you will have a well-designed professional-looking business logo created by the one who probably has been doing this for years.

It doesn't matter which option you pick from the above list, the point is to get a professional business logo in order to advertise your services. Doing so at the initial stage of your freelancing career would help you a lot in future, i.e. when you will be in the process of business expansion and trying to create a brand name as an organization.

Once you get a decent business logo designed by yourself or by any other means, you can place the logo on every page of your website/blog, and if possible, also on your profile page of the freelancing directory where you have an account. This will make you look more professional. In addition to this, you can add the logo as your email signature, and can even get some business cards with your logo printed on them to help you propagate your services among your social and professional circle.

ROLE OF WEBSITE/BLOG (PART I)

Since you are likely to get most of your business from the clients online, one of the best and most trusted ways to become visible and available globally is by getting your own website.

A website or blog shows your online existence to the people worldwide and contains all the information about your line of business, area of expertise, working hours, availability status, contact details, reviews from your existing clients (if applicable), etc.

Because it is a web address that can be accessed from all over the world via Internet, you are always within people's reach, thus enabling anyone from anywhere to contact you whenever they need your services/products. At your end, you have the flexibility of responding to the people's queries at your convenience.

Why You Need a Website or Blog?

If you have started your career as a freelancer recently, it is likely that you will be working alone, at least for the initial few months. Regardless of the scale of your business or the phase of career you are in, there must be some place where you can be easily found for communication when needed, and your website/blog serves this purpose pretty well.

Some advantages of having your own website/blog are:

➤ **Visibility**
   With your own blog/website, you can create your complete portfolio detailing all your skills and area of ex-

pertise, and can make your profile visible to anyone who visits your page.

> ## Availability

With your own website/blog, it becomes easy for your clients to locate you and communicate with you in offline mode in case you are not available on your regular communication mediums due to any reason. In addition to this, even the clients from other countries can communicate with you via your blog or website. This further increases your chances of getting more business from the foreign market as well, hence giving you a better exposure for your future references.

> ## Notices/News

On your blog/website, you can share important notifications. For example, the duration when you'll be on vacation and won't be able to respond to the clients' mails or phone calls. In addition to this, if you have updated your skillset in any field, you can mention that on your site too.

> ## Discount Offers

You can even use your website to throw attractive discount offers to the existing or new visitors. For instance, you can offer 10% discount on the first project your new clients award you, or 15% discount for any project that costs $1000 USD or above. This can be yet another way of getting more business from your clients.

> ## Feedbacks

On your website, you can and you MUST create a separate 'Feedback' column where your existing clients can leave comments about their experience working with you. Such feedbacks help you improve your skills and also enable the new clients to assess your efficiency. This further encourages them to award you with the projects.

The list of benefits is endless, but the idea behind it is simple. Get your website and populate it with as much details as possible.

How to Get Your Website?

The entire process consists of multiple steps:

> **Domain Name**

The first thing you need is a domain name. A domain name is your web name using which people will be able to locate you online. There are various domain registrars who allow you to search for your preferred domain and register it in your name at nominal annual subscription cost. Since no two domain names can be identical, make sure to think of something that is unique and explains your business well.

> **Web Hosting**

Once you have registered your domain, you need a web hosting to hold your website files and also has your domain name attached to it. Web hosting can be purchased on monthly or annual subscription basis. Also, these service providers offer various hosting plans to choose from, and you can pick the one that best fits your needs and remains within your budget.

Since most web hosting service providers nowadays allow you to search for and register a domain name from their site, your need of registering a domain from a domain registrar separately is eliminated. Also, many hosting providers even let you register a domain name for free if you pick any of their web hosting plans.

> **Website**

Your website consists of multiple webpages that are displayed on the screen of the site visitors. There are many programming languages that can be used to develop a website, and the one you pick to build yours depends on the type of site you want to have, and the features you want to add to it.

If you are not much into programming, and are planning to hire a professional web developer to build a website for you, you may need to explain your requirements to him in detail before he starts working on your site.

On the other hand, as a new freelancer if you don't want to invest funds in registering a domain, getting a website developed, and hosting it online, you can use any of the free blogging websites that allow you to sign-up on their domains and create your own blog without any cost and with no technical skills. Since such sites offer free services, although they may not have advanced tools for you to work with, the ones they provide are sufficient enough to set up your blog quickly and easily with all the options required by you.

ROLE OF UPDATES (PART II)

Even the purest water gets infected if it has no movement in it.

Regular activities in any object are mandatory to keep it live, and same is the case with your website/blog/portfolio and even your own personality.

In order to keep rolling and to let people know that you are professionally active, you should regularly update your portfolio/website/blog by posting new and unique information on it. With continuous updates, your clients would know that you are:

> ➤ **Available**
>
> You look active when you regularly update your blog or site with new information, discount offers, or your current working status. This allows your clients to know your availability, and helps them pick the right time to communicate with you.

> ➤ **Within Reach**
>
> With your regular activities/updates on your blog/website, clients can know that you are still there and will respond whenever they approach you.

> ➤ **Sincere Toward Work**
>
> If you love your job, you will always be involved in it, and get it done with efficiency and perfection. This is what your regular updates on your blog/site reflect about you. With the updates, the viewers can see how much you are into your profession. This further encourages them to rely upon you and award you the projects.

In addition to the above advantages, regularly updating your website or blog also helps you remain in touch with your work even if you are out of projects for a while.

Planning Your Weeks

Success comes to those who plan each step before they act upon it.

If you are looking for a long term career as a freelancer, it is important to plan and schedule the workdays of a week a day before the previous week ends.

For example, you must plan each day of the second week of the month on Friday or Saturday of the first week of that month. This way you will always know what you are supposed to do on which day of the upcoming week. This approach further saves your time, keeps your mind at peace, and allows you to focus on the prescheduled tasks instead of getting lost in the messed up unscheduled hours.

Also, planning your next week's tasks at the end of every week helps you become more systematic, disciplined, and synchronized when it comes to completing your assignments by the deadlines, or sometimes even before the completion date. There are a few direct and indirect advantages of this approach, namely:

Direct Benefits

➤ **Timely Project Completion**
Since a big project is divided into several parts when it is in process, with the prescheduled weekdays every week, you know the deadline for every part of the assignment you are working on. This enables you to complete the entire project on, or sometimes before time.

> **Reputation**
> With the timely completed projects, you can make your clients glad and fully satisfied. This would further encourage them to reward you with good feedbacks.

> **More Business**
> With good reputation and decent feedbacks, your chances of getting more business from your existing and new clients are remarkably increased.

Indirect Benefits

> **Manage Other Things**
> When you schedule your time properly, you can easily take out some for your family and friends, and can also participate in other social affairs.

> **Time for Recreation and Fitness**
> With well-planned and scheduled workdays, you also save some time for your relaxation and recreation, and even to join some health clubs to stay fit and in good physical shape.

To sum up, with the planned workdays, as an indirect benefit, you ultimately get a scheduled lifestyle that can help you live longer, and with peace and joy. Once you are in the habit of planning your every step, with a fully disciplined life, you can easily reach the heights of success soon, thus completing your journey toward becoming a successful entrepreneur in lesser time.

Once you are an entrepreneur, this disciplined life will help you manage your business, organization, manpower, and other important factors of your business efficiently.

JOTTING

As with the ocean waves, since the new ideas come to your mind at one instance and get washed away in another, you must jot them down in order to make it easy for you to recall them later.

It is a good practice to carry a small notebook and pen along with you while you are on the move. This will help you jot down the ideas that hit your mind instantaneously, and will also allow you to note any important information or contact details of the new people who you get introduced with unexpectedly.

Since most new ideas come to the mind when it is fresh and free from tensions, having a notebook with you every time will enable you to keep everything written down safely, from where you can extract the required information whenever needed.

Advantages of Writing Over Typing

Even if you are used to working on a PC and your fingers move more swiftly on the keyboard as compared to handling a pen, the traditional way of jotting down the important stuff can never become obsolete.

A few reasons why you should prefer writing down your important notes and new ideas in your notebook instead of memorizing or typing them on your computer are:

> ➤ **Productive Mind**
>   Your mind automatically becomes more innovative and can come up with better ideas when you hold a pen to

write. Also, writing those ideas in your notebook saves them on the paper forever.

> **Less Errors**

Because your mind is completely focused on the ideas you wish to jot down, your chances of making any errors or forgetting any of your thoughts are remarkably reduced.

> **Increased Creativity**

As discussed above, when you write, you are able to come up with the better ideas. This creativity of your mind helps you produce quality output. In addition to this, if you had any idea before that skipped your mind, while writing, you can recall those innovations comparatively easily.

> **Helps in Memorizing**

It is well-known that when you write something, you memorize it easily, and therefore are able to recall things more quickly. This is contrary to typing on the keyboard.

> **Mental Relaxation**

Once you are done writing, you get the feeling of having transferred all the burden off your shoulders on to the paper. This enables you to work more freely and produce better output.

Benefits of a Whiteboard

While on the move, although you can use a notepad to jot down the key things that you want to remember, when in office, having a whiteboard hanging on a wall of your room will always motivate you to leave your chair every now and then to write important notes, or to make or modify the to-do lists there.

Furthermore, according to a latest research, in the long run, a desk-bound lifestyle can lead to:

> Various heart diseases

> Diabetes

> Cancer

> Other physical disabilities

Therefore, before you start working as a freelancer where you will be spending most of your time sitting on your desk, make sure to set a routine where you can get up from your chair from time-to-time in order to stay healthy, keep your mind fresh, and to avoid monotonous working behavior/environment. A whiteboard can help you in that.

To elaborate, the habit of writing on whiteboard will help you in the following ways:

> **Physical Fitness**

Because you will be moving yourself frequently, i.e. getting up from your chair and walking all the way to the whiteboard to write things down, you will remain physically active throughout the day and will also remain free from any side effects or health issues that are caused by having a desk-bound lifestyle.

> **Proper Schedule Following**

When you are in a habit of writing your to-do lists on a whiteboard, you see the current day's list every time you raise up your head from your files or computer screen. This way, you are always aware of the tasks that you have planned to do, and which ones you are supposed pick up in the next hour.

> **Comfortable Conferencing**

If you happen to arrange a meeting of your allies or clients at your office, a whiteboard would allow you to explain things in a better, more informative manner. You can draw diagrams and even demonstrate your ideas graphically on the board.

> **Reflect Professionalism**

A hanging whiteboard on one of the walls of your room would give your work area a professional look that will further put a positive impact on the office visitors, including the local clients who visit your workplace to discuss the assignments.

To summarize, make it a habit to write your important stuff regularly. Your preference should be to use a good quality whiteboard and marker in your office instead of a notebook unless you are on the move. This will encourage you to move away from your desk several times during your working hours.

MONTHLY INVESTMENTS

After all it's your business that will be (or probably it already is by now) paying you well and giving you a luxurious and lavish life. Right?

The more you love your business and take good care of it, the more will it reward you with good amount of cash and fame.

The fact is, your business will grow as much as you invest in it. The term 'investment' is quite broad and covers many aspects such as:

> Time

> Devotion

> Funds

> Skills

> Mind

However, this title relates to the funds. ;)

That being said, if you have started your career as a freelancer and if you are good at what you do, you will start earning a good sum of money pretty soon. Once this happens, make sure to invest at least 15% to 25% of your monthly profit in your business for its expansion.

A few areas where you may want to invest some percentage of your monthly profit include:

> **Licensed Applications**
   Since licensed applications have many advanced features that their free alternatives don't, you can invest some percentage of your profit to purchase a licensed

copy of any of the mission-critical software that you believe would make your task easier, and help you expedite the process while working on the projects.

> If there are multiple applications that you work on, it would be good to buy at least one every month until you have purchased the licenses of all the mission-critical programs.

> **Important Accessories**

You can also invest a small percentage of your monthly benefit to gather additional accessories that can help you in your day-to-day business needs. Such accessories can be:

→ A spare hard disk drive

→ A decent quality optical mouse

→ A smooth keyboard

→ A good quality headphone/microphone/speaker system

→ A multi-tasking printing device

→ Additional USB drives

→ A comfortable and good looking furniture, etc.

> **Hire Someone**

On a bit increased scale, i.e. when you start earning a decent amount of funds, you can hire an assistant who can help you in completing other simple but time consuming tasks such as formatting your documents to make them look professional, rearranging your data, setting up your computer and activating the copies of the licensed software, etc.

Although it would be a regular investment to hire an assistant as you have to pay him/her monthly salary, with a helping hand you can save a good amount of time that you can utilize to bid for and work on more projects to generate more business.

As you can notice, the above list majorly discusses about the computer related stuff. This is because as a freelancer, you are likely to do most of your tasks on your computer, and the suggestions given above can help in making things easier for you. However, if you belong to a different field, by all means you can invest funds in buying the relevant accessories that can help you with your business.

Savings are Important Too

In addition to investing some part of your monthly profit in your business, saving the funds is equally important. Not only your savings would give you potential to scale up your business significantly in near future, they will also make you confident, intellectual, and resourceful.

Your business needs your complete and undistracted devotion, especially when it is at its early stage. With such motherly care toward your work, and, of course with regular top-notch performance in your projects, you will become a successful businessperson in no time.

UNIT 6
MANAGING STRESS

Scope of This Unit

At any stage of your business, you are likely to do many tasks simultaneously to keep things running. With continuous work and wearisome schedule, you may start leading a stressful life without even noticing it.

Although a brief one, this unit tells how you can plan your weekdays and weekends to avoid monotonous lifestyle and remain fresh and stress-free throughout the day, every day.

Borrowing Time

Y ou are the most important person in your life. Isn't it?

Since you love yourself, try to avoid indulging yourself in your work continuously for long hours as it may increase stress, reduce your efficiency and productivity, and you may even face some health issues in the long run. Instead, you must do your best to remain happy, energetic, positive, and healthy.

Because it is practically not possible for you to work for 24 hours a day, 7 days a week, and 365 days a year, in order to remain fresh, relaxed, and efficient in your work, it is important to schedule your day in such a way that you get some time for yourself, failing to which you may end up having stressful personal and professional lives.

Below are a few suggestions that can help you balance your lifestyle properly:

During the weekdays you should:

➤ **Talk to Family**

Whatever you are doing and anything that you'll do in future will be to make your family happy. Therefore, despite of being occupied with your assignments and other professional things, make sure to spend some time of your day with your family. This will not only help you see the current activities your family is engaged with but will also keep you connected to them and make you and the family members feel relaxed.

> **Relax and Rest**

You can't work continuously even during your working hours as it may block your mind, leave you out of ideas soon, and will gradually decrease your efficiency. Therefore, whenever possible, take a short break, rest for a while, and let your brain relax. (These breaks should be in addition to your lunch and tea breaks.) A few things that you may consider doing during those short breaks can be:

→ Have a cup of coffee

→ Play a refreshing game on your mobile or computer

→ Take a brief walk within your room or outside

→ Listen to your favorite music

> **Be Social**

As with your family, it is equally important to remain in touch with your friends and relatives too. Therefore, you should try to take out some time from your busy schedule and communicate with them often.

During the weekends you should:

> **Wear Lose Casuals**

You might be wearing decent and tight-fitting cloths throughout the week while working but at the weekends, you should prefer wearing as lose cloths as possible. Doing so will help you feel more relaxed and free from all the work pressure.

> **Do Your Hobby**

Since it's weekend, you have all the time in the world to do what you love the most. For instance, if you love painting, grab a brush and a canvas board and start drawing a sketch. This will give you utmost pleasure and mental relaxation.

➤ **Avoid Official Communication**

Since the weekends are your personal days that you should spend relaxing and enjoying quality time with your family and friends, avoiding any kind of official communication like emails, phone calls, etc. won't be wrong.

➤ **Sleep Well**

Because you have been working tirelessly for the whole week, it is your right to take good rest, and nothing can serve the purpose better than having a tight snoring sleep.

➤ **Recreate**

You can even go shopping or picnic with your family or friends or both.

Following the above points during the weekends will keep your mind fresh, and will make you more productive and efficient when you return back to your work the next week.

Also, with the suggestions given above as how should you plan your weekdays and weekends, you can easily manage both your professional and personal lives, and can effectively maintain a proper balance between the two.

Inhale Fresh Air

Apart from following different routines in weekdays and weekends, this is something that you should do more often.

Since inhaling fresh air keeps you in good mental and physical shape, while preparing your daily schedule, do not forget to include some time in which you can go out for a walk to refresh yourself. You should follow this practice at least once in every 24 to 48 hours.

Your preference should be to go for a walk early morning, every day. Since the air is fresh and free from any pollution in the morning time, with this practice, you feel refreshed and energetic. If you are not in a habit of waking up early, evening walks can serve the purpose well too.

The idea is, you should not always remain at home/office breathing within its walls as a prisoner. By leaving your place for some time each day, even if it is for short duration, you will remain mentally fit and balanced, and will stay away from any stresses. This will further help you come up with innovative ideas to complete your tasks more efficiently and productively.

Always remember, your journey to become an entrepreneur is lot more demanding than you can imagine, and at times you may feel stressed or overburdened with work. Make sure you maintain the habit of taking out some time for your social life and recreations. This will keep you calm, balanced, disciplined, and in proper mental shape. Once you are a successful entrepreneur and are involved in too many things in order to keep your business running, this habit will work as a boon to give you a healthy and stress-free lifestyle.

Notes

Notes